Inventions That Shaped the World

The Telescope

T A M R A   O R R

Franklin Watts
A Division of Scholastic Inc.
New York • Toronto • London • Auckland • Sydney
Mexico City • New Delhi • Hong Kong
Danbury, Connecticut

Photographs © 2004: AKG-Images, London: 13, 33, 50, 54; AP/Wide World Photos/Robert P. Mathews/Princeton University: 65; Art Resource, NY/Victoria and Albert Museum, London, Great Britain: 8; Bridgeman Art Library International Ltd., London/New York: 7 (Bibliotheque Municipale, Boulogne sur Mer, France), 26 (Lauros/Giraudon/Musee National des Techniques, Paris, France), chapter openers, 57 (Royal Society, London, UK), 9 (The Stapleton Collection/ Topkapi Palace Museum, Istanbul, Turkey), cover left, 22 (Ken Welsh/Private Collection), 14, 35; Corbis Images: cover right, 11 (Archivo Iconografico, S.A.), 17, 19, 23, 25, 29, 52 (Bettmann), cover bottom, 64 (NASA), 39, 60 right (Roger Ressmeyer), 45 (Roger Ressmeyer/NASA), 67 (Reuters NewMedia Inc.), 41 (Stapleton Collection), 46; Corbis Sygma: 69; Culver Pictures: 15, 56; Hulton|Archive/Getty Images: 30; Institute and Museum of the History of Science, Firenze, Italy/Franca Principe: 31; NASA: 66 (J.P. Harrington & K.J. Borkowski), 68 (HubbleSite/ Northrop Grumman); North Wind Picture Archives: 48, 51; Photo Researchers, NY: 16 (Dr. Jeremy Burgess/SPL), 63 (Hale Observatories), 27, 58, 60 left (SPL); PhotoEdit: 5 (Tony Freeman), 61 (Jonathan Nourok); Stock Montage, Inc.: 55.

Cover design by Kathleen Santini
Book production by Jeff Loppacker

Library of Congress Cataloging-in-Publication Data

Orr, Tamra.
    The telescope / Tamra Orr.
        p. cm. — (Inventions that shaped the world)
    Summary: Describes the invention of the telescope, the impact it has had on modern culture, and the patterns of change that resulted from its discovery and use.
Includes bibliographical references and index.
        ISBN 0-531-12344-8 (lib. bdg.)   0-531-16736-4 (pbk.)
1. Telescope—Juvenile literature. [1. Telescopes—History.] I. Title. II. Series.
        QB88.O77 2004
        522'.2—dc22   2003015208

Contents

The Mysteries of the Sky

Have you ever looked up into the sky and wondered what was out there? Perhaps one object twinkles brighter or is a different color than the others. Could it be a planet? Have you looked through a telescope and seen things up close and marveled at what you saw? You are not alone in your wonder. What lies beyond the clouds and sky has been one of the longest and most lasting mysteries throughout history. From the twinkling

People of all ages are fascinated by what mysteries await discovery in the sky.

5

stars of the *constellations* to the deep secrets of distant planets and countless *galaxies*, the universe attracts and interests people of all ages, all over the world. Thanks to continual research and new discoveries, humankind knows quite a bit about the wonders of the universe surrounding Earth. Earth's solar system contains the Sun, along with nine planets and their moons and various asteroids and comets. People now know that when we look up into the sky and see constellations, these stars are part of the Milky Way Galaxy, which consists of billions of stars. We also realize that the Milky Way is only one of the many galaxies that fill the universe.

Much is known about how the planets move and appear. For example, science has proven that planets rotate, or turn on their axes as they revolve around the Sun. While stars may look the same from a distance, they actually vary greatly in size, temperature, brightness, and age. The last century of scientific exploration has given people a better look at some of the planets. Satellite images are transmitted to homes around the world, giving us glimpses of the surface of the Moon, showing that Saturn has rings, and proving that Mars clearly is a red planet.

Ancient Ideas

Information about the universe is now well known, but once it was a complete mystery. Ancient cultures had many different theories about what they saw above them. Some

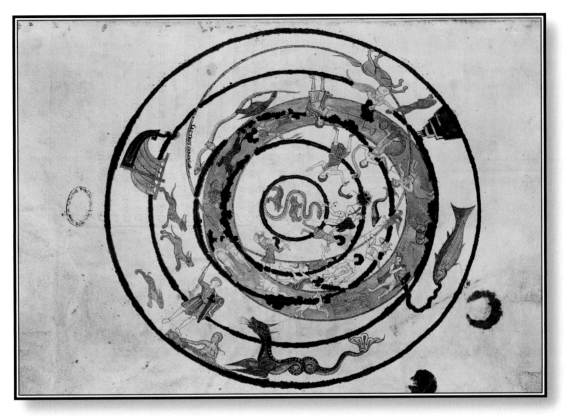

Greek philosopher, astronomer, and mathematician Eudoxus drew this illustration supporting Plato's theory of the rotation of planets around Earth.

imagined that the souls of their gods, chiefs, or leaders were looking down on them from above. The ancients looked up into the night sky with both fear and fascination. Some worshipped what they could see in the sky. Others ignored it all. It was not until around 600 B.C. that Greek philosophers and scientists began to come up with some theories about what really did lie beyond the clouds.

Eudoxus of Cnidus was a Greek who lived about 370 B.C. He developed a mechanical system that showed how each of the planets moved. He told others that everything in the solar system revolved around Earth. This was called a *geocentric*, or Earth-centered, idea. It was a theory that many agreed with and would continue to for years. One of the most outspoken followers of this geocentric theory was a second-century A.D. Greek astronomer and geographer named Claudius Ptolemaeus. He drew images of Earth at the

This illustration shows the motions of the heavens as envisioned by Claudius Ptolemaeus.

center of the solar system with the Sun and other heavenly bodies revolving around it. His illustrations made the concept seem more real to people, and it was not long before these ideas came to be called the Ptolemaic System.

In the 300s B.C., a Greek philosopher named Aristotle took up the idea of a geocentric system in which Earth was viewed as the center of all things. He taught many others about it.

Aristotle was considered one of the two most important philosophers in history.

Aristotle had a lot of influence in his time. People listened to him closely and believed what he had to say. He had a great many theories about a number of things. Some of them were amazingly correct. Others were just as amazingly wrong. Not only did he believe that everything revolved around Earth, he thought that Earth itself did not move in any way. According to Aristotle, Earth was the center point of all creation. He thought that it operated under a set of physical laws that were different from the ones that directed everything else in space.

In addition to that, Aristotle taught his students that philosophy, as opposed to direct observation or experimentation, was what decided the actual truth about things. He stated that pure thoughts should not be questioned or tested in any way. They were just to be accepted. In addition, Aristotle, although a supporter of reasoning and logic, sometimes applied his thoughts and ideals in ways that slowed down the scientific process. He was, after all, a philosopher and not a scientist. He believed that the world was perfectly symmetrical, and he refused to allow this belief to be questioned or tested.

The Role of the Church

For hundreds of years, Aristotle's philosophy was followed. As the centuries rolled by, the Catholic Church in Greece and other areas began to gain power. They liked the theory, too. They felt Aristotle's ideas of a perfect planet and heavenly bodies were further proof of God's presence and the perfection of all He created. Anyone who dared to speak out against church policy risked being tortured, thrown into prison, or even killed.

In 1473, Nicolaus Copernicus was born in Poland. He would be one of the leading thinkers to challenge Aristotle's and the church's ideas. He did not agree that concepts were not to be tested, but accepted. Copernicus set out to create a more exact description of the universe. He concluded that the Sun, not the Earth, was the center of the solar system, a *heliocentric* philosophy. He stated that all the planets, including Earth, revolved around the Sun. The Roman Catholic Church was stunned and furious. This idea did not fit in with either Aristotle's theories or the church's belief that God had made Earth the center of creation.

One person who believed that Copernicus was right was a scientist by the name

Fourteenth-century illuminated manuscript featuring an illustration of an astronomer using equipment to look into the sky.

of Galileo Galilei (1564–1642). He wanted to find a way to prove that Copernicus's theory was correct. His quest to do this and the incredible invention he used to do so changed the way the world viewed the solar system from then on. The telescope would bring the mysterious universe closer and clearer for all to see.

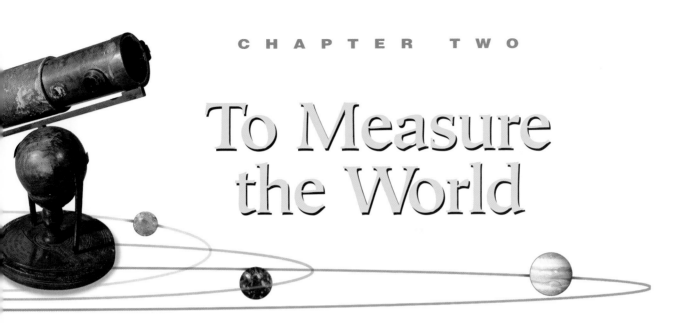

To Measure the World

In Europe during the mid-fourteenth to the late sixteenth centuries, a new era began called the *Renaissance*. Renaissance means rebirth in French and indicated a renewed interest in art, education, and science. It was a rich time in history when invention, science, and art became passions for many. During this period people began to wonder more about how the world worked, yet there were very few answers to their questions. Philosophers started looking more closely at nature

The Renaissance was a time of questioning. Here people are becoming increasingly interested in astronomy.

and attempted to structure and measure the natural world for the first time. Inventions came along to help them at an amazing pace.

Very soon inventions such as the first thermometer for measuring temperature and the barometer for measuring the weight of the atmosphere, which helped with weather forecasting, were introduced. Other incredible inventions included the first clock that gave an accurate measurement of time and the microscope, an instrument that allowed physicians to see the tiny inner workings of things.

Flemish **cartographer**, or mapmaker, Gerardus Mercator drew a map of the entire world in 1569. It was an enormous

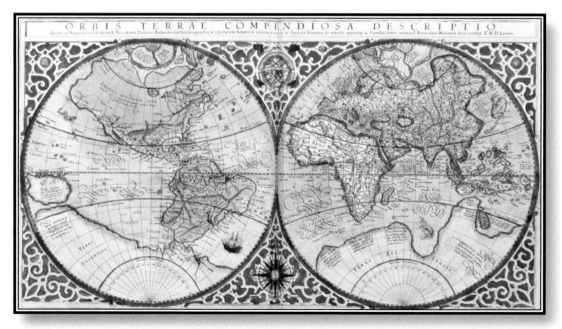

Maps by cartographer Mercatur expanded people's minds as they realized how big the world really was.

A BLAZE IN THE SKY

In late 1572, hundreds of eyes turned upward in awe to watch a *nova* blaze across the sky in the middle of a constellation known as Cassiopeia. It was incredibly bright and could even be seen in the daytime. It burned like that for two years. Its appearance was fascinating to some, but worrisome to others. They had no way to explain it. The Bible taught that God had completed the universe in seven days. At the end of the

week, He was finished, and the world was done. So how could there possibly be a new star in the sky? Where did it come from? Not only was it something that had never appeared before, it was also farther away than anything else that had been observed, impossibilities according to the doctrine of the church. That puzzle was only added to five years later when a very bright comet was spotted crossing the sky. The church tried to explain it as something related to the weather, like a rainbow, but many questioned the church's explanation. Much to the annoyance of the church, the desire to find out exactly what the universe was made of began to increase.

aid in navigation. Although the distances between places were frequently incorrect, the map was still a huge step toward understanding the positions of the continents. The Mercator style of mapping proved so useful that it is still used today.

Each one of these creations helped people to see their world in new ways and to have a better, clearer understanding of how Earth worked. As mystery and myth faded, knowledge increased.

An Accident in the Workshop

One of the men who helped invent something that would eventually answer these wonderings was a Dutch eyeglass maker named Hans Lippershey (1570–1619). Born in Wesel, Germany, Lippershey lived most of his life in Middleburg, the capital city of Zeeland in the Netherlands.

There are two legends about how Lippershey first hit upon the idea of creating an instrument that would enable a person to see far distances. One version states that a young apprentice in Lippershey's workshop picked up a glass lens, held it to his eye, and then placed another

Hans Lippershey is a little recognized name, yet he was the first person to imagine the possibility of a telescope.

lens an arm's length away. The apprentice noticed that a church tower in the distance appeared to be much closer than it actually was. He hurried to tell his boss what he had discovered. The other story is similar, except that two small children who were playing in the workshop made the discovery. Two lenses happened to be lined up. The children glanced through them to see, once again, the very same church tower, appearing to be quite near. Regardless of how it happened, Lippershey was suddenly struck with

Hans Lippershey's workshop was where the first glimpse of a telescope began.

the possibility of "an instrument for seeing at a distance." He thought it would be a perfect piece of equipment for warfare. Troops armed with these devices would be able to know far sooner when the enemy approached and be able to spot traps long before they reached them. The invention came to be known as a spyglass. With this invention, Lippershey saw the chance to become rich and famous, so he wanted to keep it top secret until he had a *patent*. That ended up being impossible to obtain.

Lippershey sent a letter to the government of Zeeland on September 25, 1608, asking officials to "help the bearer who claims to have a certain device by means of which all things at a very great distance can be seen as if they were nearby by looking through glasses which he claims to be a new invention." The letter was sent in the hopes that Lippershey would be given a patent for the device, ensuring that he would get sole credit for the invention. In order to be given a patent, he was required to make three more models of the device, as well as keep the process secret. He did make other models, and for that he was paid rather well. Keeping it secret, however, proved to be much more difficult.

Here Comes Competition

Word leaked out quickly about this new piece of equipment, and soon after Lippershey had applied for a patent, a man named Jacob (sometimes called James) Metius filed his

COPERNICUS'S CONTRIBUTION

One of the scientists who most inspired Galileo was Polish astronomer Mikolaj Kopernik, better known as Nicolaus Copernicus. In 1514, Copernicus was asked by the pope to help create a more accurate calendar. Existing calendars were flawed and could not be improved until there was a bet-

ter prediction of star positions. Copernicus stated that this would be impossible until the actual relationship between the Sun and the Moon was resolved. He accepted neither the church's nor Aristotle's explanation of how the solar system was put together, with Earth in the center.

In May of the same year, Copernicus wrote a paper called *The Little Commentary* in which he explained his theory that the Sun, not the Earth, is at the center of the solar system. He also stated that he thought the Earth revolved around the Sun, just as the other planets did. That paper was not actually published until just before Copernicus's death in 1543 and was renamed *On the Revolution of the Celestial Spheres*. Copernicus was afraid that his words would be misunderstood. He also knew that his concepts would create rage and denial within the church. His ideas shattered the illusion that God created the heavens for mankind alone.

own patent request for the very same invention. The government turned both men down because it was obvious that information about the instrument had been leaked. The secret was out.

After Metius was turned away, history says that he remained very protective of his invention. He never showed it to another person, and upon his death, all of the tools he had used to make his device were destroyed. Amazingly, thirty years later, a third man applied for a patent for the same instrument. His name was Zacharias Janssen.

One person who had heard rumors of an instrument that could allow a person to see long distances was the Italian scientist Galileo Galilei. He was a man driven by the need to understand things and had already performed a number of fascinating experiments by the early 1600s. When he first heard of Lippershey's invention, his thoughts were not of warfare but of how such a device might help him answer one of his most persistent questions—What was really out there in the sky? Could this new equipment somehow be improved and refined enough to give scientists the greatest opportunity of all—to look up into the skies and beyond to see the planets and stars? He suspected that it might and that he would be the person to find out for sure.

CHAPTER THREE

The Starry Messenger

The man who one day would be called "the father of modern science" was born in the region of Pisa, Italy, on February 15, 1564. Although he was a very bright child, no one could have guessed that he would grow up to be one of the most influential inventors in the world, as well as a mathematician, astronomer, physicist, and philosopher.

The Family Galilei

Galileo Galilei was the firstborn child of Vincenzo Galilei, a cloth merchant and musician, and Giulia Ammannati. Two brothers and four sisters followed. Until Galileo was eleven years old, he was educated at home by his father. He was then sent to the Benedictine monastery of Santa Maria di Vallombrosa near Florence, Italy. There he studied

Galileo Galilei earned several titles during his life including father of modern physics, father of modern astronomy, and father of science.

Latin, Greek, religion, music, and art. However, when he began to show an interest in becoming a monk, Vincenzo sent him to the University of Pisa, hoping that he would eventually become a doctor. After years of struggling to raise his large family on the small earnings of a musician, Vincenzo wished more for his son financially.

During his early years at Pisa, Galileo made one of his first important discoveries. While sitting in the university's cathedral, a breeze blew through. Galileo noticed that the lamps hanging from the ceiling were being blown back and forth. He began to time their swinging with his own heartbeat and found that, regardless of the size of the lamp, each swing took exactly the same amount of time. This concept brought him instant recognition in the academic world and laid the groundwork for a Dutch mathematician and physicist named Christian Huygens to create a *pendulum*. That pendulum would be used to regulate clocks for the next 250 years.

Although Galileo invented the pendulum, a clock using his design was not built until after his death.

Galileo had been at Pisa for four years when he learned that his family could not afford to pay his tuition any longer. Although scholarships were available, none was given to Galileo. He received excellent grades, but he was not an easy student to have in a classroom because he questioned so many things and argued against anything that could not be proven. He earned himself the nickname "the Wrangler" because of it.

Galileo left the University of Pisa and let his father know that a career in medicine was not what he really wanted. Instead, he wanted to study the components of physics: matter, energy, motion, and force. He began to learn more about physics from a mathematics professor and family friend, Ostillio Ricci.

The Wrangler Moves On

Even though he was not able to graduate from the University of Pisa, Galileo was hired as a professor there in 1589. Although things started out smoothly, the job didn't last long. Galileo went back to challenging old rules and theories. He decided to prove that Aristotle's theory that heavier objects fall faster than lighter ones do was false. Supposedly, he climbed to the top of the Tower of Pisa and, in front of a crowd of curious students and disapproving professors, dropped two balls of different sizes and weights. As he had theorized, they landed at the exact same time.

Galileo questioned everything. Here he sets out to prove that the weight of an object does not affect its speed.

Despite what they had just seen, many professors refused to accept it. When Galileo's teaching contract expired, it was not renewed.

Not sure what to do next, Galileo decided to go to the University of Padua, another region in what would one day be Italy, and teach there instead. He continued to experiment with different elements while he was there and created one of the first thermometers. He met a woman in Padua, fell in love, and started a family. When his father passed away, being the eldest, Galileo had to take on the responsibility for his younger brothers and sisters. To help support

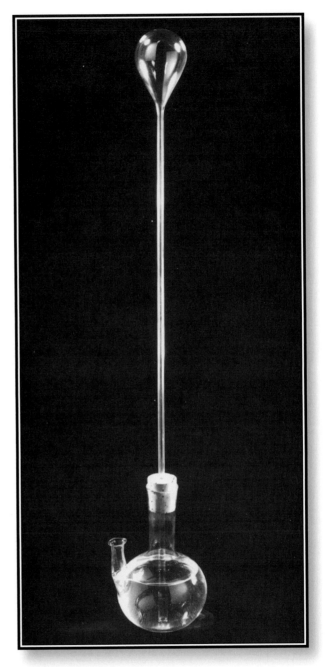

The thermoscope was one of Galileo's first temperature telling devices.

THE GALILEO FAMILY

Galileo never married, though he did have a family. In 1599, at the age of thirty-five, he met Marina Gamba. The two were together for twelve years and had three children. Their first child was a daughter named Virginia, born in August of 1600. Their second daughter, Livia, was born in August of 1601. The last child, a son named Vincenzo, was born in August of 1606.

Both of Galileo's daughters became nuns. In the convent, Livia was renamed Sister Arcangela, and Virginia (pictured) was renamed Sister Maria Celeste. As an adult, Virginia and her father had a close relationship.

Many of the letters she wrote to him have survived, and they show the affection and respect she had for her father.

When Galileo returned to Florence, his daughters went with him, but Vincenzo was left with Gamba. Vincenzo did join his father several years later, and when he was almost thirteen, Galileo officially claimed him as his son for the first time. In Galileo's last years of life, Vincenzo was often at his father's side, and they became very close.

them and provide dowries for his sisters, which are gifts of money or property given to grooms, Galileo took several part-time jobs, including tutoring students in his home and running a store that sold compasses and other scientific equipment. Galileo's reputation continued to grow, and students came from all over Europe to hear him lecture and watch him perform experiments. In his later writings he referred to his years in Padua as the happiest of his entire life.

An Intriguing Inspiration

In 1609, while on vacation in Venice, Galileo heard rumors about Lippershey's spyglass invention. He was intrigued. He wrote, "A report reached my ears that a certain Fleming had constructed a spyglass. . . . Upon hearing the news, I set myself to thinking about the problem. . . . Finally, sparing neither labor nor expense, I succeeded in constructing for myself so excellent an instrument that objects seen by means of it appeared nearly 1,000 times larger and over 30 times closer than when regarded with our natural vision." In a short twenty-four hours, forty-five-year-old Galileo was able to create his own spyglass, despite the fact that he had never seen the original and had only snippets of information to go on. Soon he was making and selling spyglasses. He sold his information to the government to be used as a military device. However, he certainly had different plans for its use. These plans had nothing to do with weaponry either.

Galileo's first telescope was able to magnify objects three times. His later models increased that magnification quickly.

The Word Begins to Spread

What truly set Galileo apart from all the others was his decision to turn his spyglass toward the sky. As far as we know, he was the first to do so. He realized that while seeing far distances was useful on land, it was amazing in the sky.

Galileo Galilei spent many hours staring upward, trying to identify everything he saw.

The Moon looked different than people at the time had thought. It was not a perfectly smooth, shiny sphere, but a rough one covered in mountains, valleys, and craters. He saw things he had not expected to see that altered the course of

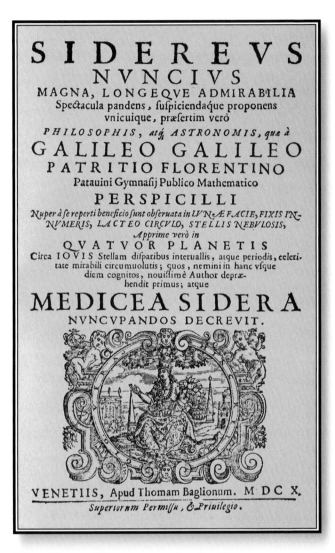

The Starry Messenger *by Galileo was a best-seller, but one that greatly upset the church.*

his life. He wanted to know what else might be out there that he was not aware of. It also motivated him to reexamine, and ultimately to agree with, the Copernican System once again. The multitude of stars he saw in the galaxy proved to him that the universe was not finite, or with definite limits, as once thought. Later, the occurrence of another supernova and his discovery of moons orbiting Jupiter strengthened his belief in the Copernican System. With this theory, everything fit and made sense to him. In 1610, Galileo wrote *The Starry Messenger*, a small book detailing some of the things he had discovered about the universe. Five hundred and fifty copies were printed, and it became an immediate hit.

Following his improvements on the spyglass, Galileo left Padua to go to Florence to become mathematician and philosopher to Cosimo II de Medici, the grand duke of Tuscany. It was a powerful and well-paid position for Galileo. The following year, in 1611, Galileo took the spyglass or, as he called it, the perspicillum, to Rome, where it was christened the "telescope."

Up until that point, Galileo's life had gone well. He loved his work and had had many successes. He was known far and wide. Parades had been held in his honor, and statues had been sculpted of him. Although he was aware that most of his ideas were not being accepted, he was not prepared for what lay ahead.

In 1616, Pope Paul V declared that the Copernican idea that the Sun was at the center of the solar system instead of the Earth was a lie. According to the Bible, Earth is standing still. Galileo was stunned. He knew the pope was wrong, but what was he to do? To speak out against the church was foolish and, in those days, even dangerous.

Trouble and Threats of Torture

Galileo had been right about the dangers of going up against the church. In 1624, he had traveled to Rome to meet with his former friend and supporter, Pope Paul VIII, and several cardinals. While there, the pope had given Galileo permission to write about his Copernican ideas about the solar system

SUNSPOTS OR SATELLITES

One of the men responsible for bringing negative attention to Galileo was a German Jesuit named Christoph Scheiner (pictured). He felt that he was a competitor of Galileo. He began working with telescopes in 1610, and during his research he noticed some dark marks on the surface of the Sun. He called them sunspots. Unlike Galileo, Scheiner was a firm believer in Aristotle's theories and so believed that the Sun was perfect, like everything else in the universe that God had created. The spots could not possibly be flaws, so he declared that they were satellites of the Sun, casting shadows. All his statements were based on religion and philosophy rather than on science.

Galileo disagreed immediately, and the argument grew bigger and louder. Things got worse for Galileo when a young priest named Thomas Caccini took up Scheiner's side and began delivering powerful and persuasive sermons against this new science and its leader, Galileo. The pressure mounted on Galileo, and it was not long before he received a summons to the Inquisition, which led to the tragedy that followed.

as long as he promised to treat them only as theories. He was warned not to talk about his ideas, but if he did, he was to express them as possibilities, not truths.

Galileo did his best to abide by that command, but it went against everything he believed in. When his *Dialogue on the Two Great Systems of the World* was published in 1632, it stated that the heliocentric model of the solar system was the truth. He published it in Italian rather than in Latin so that more people would be able to read it. It was a true sensation and became a best seller of its time.

Not surprisingly, Galileo was immediately summoned to Florence. The pope was upset with the scientist for putting forth his disrespectful theories, according to the church, about the solar system. The publication of the book was halted, for the pope banned the title. It would remain banned until 1822.

The pope ordered Galileo to Rome to appear before the Holy Office of the *Inquisition*. Galileo was charged with *heresy*. The charges read as follows:

Namely for having held and believed a doctrine which is false and contrary to the divine and Holy Scripture; that the sun is the center of the world and does not move from east to west and the earth moves and is not the center of the world, and that one may hold and define as probable an opinion after it has been declared and defined as contrary to the Holy Scripture.

(June 1633, Rome)

It was a difficult time for the scientist. He was pestered with repeated colds, various aches and pains, and exhaustion. His trial began on April 12, 1633, and continued until June 22. Early in the trial he was defiant. He told the court, "I do not feel obligated to believe that the same God who has endowed us with senses, reason and intellect has

The trial of Galileo was desperate and sad as this intelligent and creative man was forced to abandon the truths he had spent his life discovering.

intended [us] to forgo their use. . . . He would not require us to deny sense and reason in physical matters which are set before our eyes and minds by direct experience and necessary demonstrations."

Giving In, Giving Up

However, after being threatened for days with torture, the noble man finally dressed in the long white robes of a sinner and went down on his knees to beg for forgiveness. He said that he did not believe Copernicus's theories and that his own statements, writings, and theories were all false. He stated that he had been mistaken; the Earth did not move around the Sun after all. Following this so-called confession, according to legend, he was said to whisper, "And yet, it moves." He signed papers declaring his errors and made a promise never to speak or write of his non-conformist ideas again. It was a tragic moment for a man who truly was a scientific genius. Even sadder moments lay ahead, though.

Additional punishment came in the form of house arrest. Galileo was confined to his home in Arcetri, outside Florence. He was not to leave his house, and his visitors had to obtain permission prior to going to see him. Fortunately, he was not far from his older daughter, and that gave him some comfort. When she died the following year, however, he felt even more lost.

A BELATED APOLOGY

Sometimes it can take an incredibly long time for people to say they are sorry or admit they are wrong. In the case of the Roman Catholic Church and Galileo, it took three hundred years! Even once it started, the process was amazingly slow.

The Second Vatican Council of 1962 to 1965 was the first to bring up the issue of forgiving Galileo. In 1979 Pope John Paul II said in a speech to the Pontifical Academy of Sciences that, "theologians, scholars and historians, animated by a spirit of sincere collaboration, will study the Galileo case more deeply." Later that year, the pope acknowledged the mistake that had been made and stated that "Galileo suffered at the hands of the church."

In October 1992, Cardinal Paul Poupard presented the pope with the official findings of the Galileo study commission. It read,

From the Galileo case we can draw a lesson which is applicable today in analogous cases which arise in our times and which may arise in the future. It often happens that, beyond two partial points of view which are in contrast, there exists a wider view of things which embraces both and integrates them.

The pope's reaction to this report was to decide that Galileo's discoveries about the Sun and Earth had been divinely inspired. He said, "Galileo sensed in his scientific research the presence of the Creator who, stirring in the depths of his spirit, stimulated him, anticipating and assisting his intuitions." This truly was an apology that was a long time in coming.

Despite his circumstances, Galileo continued to think and talk about science and experiment in every way he could. Unfortunately, in 1637, a combination of cataracts and glaucoma, ailments to the eyes, caused him to go completely blind. His son and two students came to live with him and help him finish his work. His last book, *Discourses and Mathematical Demonstrations Concerning Two New Sciences*, published in 1638, was about force and motion. This book helped to lay the groundwork for future scientific developments.

Galileo died a tired, broken, and lonely man in 1642. He was brilliant and had changed the way people viewed the solar system. His theories and inventions changed the world, a legacy that will never be forgotten.

CHAPTER FOUR

To See the Stars

In 1604, a few years before the first telescope was created, the world was fascinated and puzzled by what was going on in the skies above them. Today it is clear that a *supernova*, or exploding star, was dominating the skies. More than four centuries ago it was viewed as just a large, very bright star that shone so brilliantly in the night sky that only the Moon outshone it. The same questions that had passed through many

A supernova is one of the most energetic and explosive events to occur in the sky.

people's minds in ages past returned: What is this thing in the sky? What does it mean? How can it be there in the first place? The church taught that God had finished the heavens on the seventh day, so anything new was quite impossible. No one could have guessed that an instrument that would answer all of those questions was on the very edge of being invented.

The Challenges and the Rewards

The incredible passion of scientists to know more about things that were normally too tiny or too distant to study continued to grow. The microscope had just been invented and, by the mid-1670s, a Dutch cloth merchant named Antoni van Leeuwenhoek had figured out the secret to seeing things invisible to the human eye. He improved the magnification of the microscope by making the lenses tinier and tinier. Some were as small as a raindrop. This allowed anyone who peered into a microscope to see things as much as two hundred times bigger than they actually were.

Telescopes were quite a bit different. From Lippershey's first glimpse through two lenses in his workshop to the development of a functioning and practical spyglass was a relatively quick trip. Once the device got into Galileo's hands, changes came about even faster. He helped to increase the magnification from two times to more than thirty times.

One of the biggest challenges was referred to as "light grasp." How could enough light to see an object that was millions or even billions of miles away be captured? With a microscope, if the scientist needed more light, he could just light a lamp and cast more illumination near the instrument. That certainly was not possible with a telescope! Through experimentation, Galileo had found that the larger the lens, the more light it could capture. So he began grinding bigger and bigger lenses. At first this was helpful, but as the lenses got larger, they also got thicker, and at a certain point, the thickness began to block out the light again. It was a delicate

The Celestial Atlas *by Andreas Cellarius is an artist's rendition of what astronomers might see when peering through a telescope.*

balance. He made sure to wrap the edges of each of his lenses so that no unwanted light could leak in and distort the view. Although a number of people were producing some forms of a primitive telescope, Galileo's was considered the highest quality of the period. In fact, many referred to the instrument as "Galileo's Ladder to the Sky."

The purpose of a telescope is to magnify distant objects enough so that a person can see them clearly. It does this through a rather simple combination of mirrors (reflector) or glass (refractor) and light.

Galileo used glass lenses in his telescopes. Called objective lenses, the job of the lens at the end of the telescope is to collect a lot of light from a distant object and bring that image into focus. This enables a viewer's eye to see and recognize the image. The eyepiece lens, which goes next to the viewer's eye, takes the bright light from the focal point of the objective lens and magnifies it so that a large picture comes to the retina of the eye. When the objective lens and the eyepiece lens are combined, a telescope is made. The larger the lens, the better the telescope's ability to collect light.

From Earth to Sky

When telescopes were invented, their first use was thought to be for defense and navigation. When Galileo thought to point his telescope toward the sky, what he saw amazed and shocked him. It altered the history of his own life as well as that of the world.

The Moon was the first object he examined. Although many people thought that it was a polished, smooth sphere,

TELESCOPE TERMINOLOGY

The terminology surrounding the design of telescopes can be confusing. The most commonly used terms are

concave: Lens or mirror that is curved inward, causing light to spread out

convex: Lens or mirror that curves outward, causing light to come together at a focal point

field of view: Area of the sky that can be seen through the telescope with a given eyepiece

focal length: Distance required by a lens or mirror to bring the light to a focus

focal point or focus: Point at which light from a lens or mirror comes together

aperture: Diameter of the lens; the bigger it is, the more light it lets in

magnification or power: Ability to enlarge an image

resolution: How close two objects can be and still be detected as separate objects

as Aristotle had taught, Galileo's observations did not agree. He spent hours gazing at the lunar surface and was wonderfully surprised at what he discovered. He saw craters, valleys, and mountain ranges, some even larger than those on Earth. He later wrote about what he saw: "It is a most beautiful and delightful sight to behold the body of the Moon. . . . It certainly does not possess a smooth and polished surface, but one rough and uneven, and, just like the face of the Earth itself, is everywhere full of vast *protuberances*, deep chasms and *sinuosities*."

The surface of the Moon came as a surprise to Galileo. It was nothing like he had expected.

Once Galileo had studied the Moon, he moved on to bright stars and planets, including Jupiter. Other than the Moon, Jupiter is the brightest object in the evening sky. While observing that planet, he noticed something odd. He saw four black dots very close to the planet that he at first thought were just marks on Jupiter itself. Then he thought they might be fixed stars. After watching them at the same time each night, however, he realized that these spots moved in a regular pattern and that one or more would disappear and then reappear later. After months of watching and charting what he saw, he came to the conclusion that those spots were actually moons and that they were *orbiting* Jupiter just like Earth's Moon orbits around it. He was correct. He named them the Medicean Stars, in honor of the Florentine duke he worked for, but today they are known as the Galilean satellites (or moons) Io, Europa, Ganymede, and Callisto. The amazing discovery of these moons and how they orbited Jupiter brought him fame at first, followed by terrible trouble with the church.

Galileo would have been amazed to know that besides the four moons he discovered (above), Jupiter had dozens of smaller ones.

CHAPTER FIVE

Coping with the Heretic's Impact

The invention of the telescope was more than just the addition of a new scientific device. It was the beginning of a vast change in the way people thought about the world. At first the church tolerated these new ideas coming from such people as Galileo as irrelevant fantasies, but as these theories became more popular and the works written about them more widely read, the church changed its mind. Too many people were asking too many questions. It was time to put a stop to such ridiculous ideas before they began to erode the church's power.

Galileo's trial and punishment frightened many other scientists in Italy. The harshness of it was intimidating. Philosophers and scientists understood this threat, and the church boldly and proudly sent the news throughout

Trials, or inquisitions, were experienced by philosophers and scientists who supported Galileo.

all of Italy. Those in power who had played a part in assisting or supporting Galileo found themselves scolded, fired, and even exiled. Galileo was the church's cruel example of what could happen if scientists persisted in investigating theories that went against its doctrine. Church leaders also changed their position on scientific investigation. They now stated that it would be approved only if it was based on the assumptions of Aristotle and contained nothing at all that could in any way contradict the Scriptures.

A PUBLICATION OF IMPORTANCE

The publication of Galileo's *The Starry Messenger* in 1610 was important. Copies were sent to all the kings and princes of Europe and quickly earned Galileo the prestigious title of Chief Philosopher and Mathematician to the Medici court.

The introduction to his book shows his intense pride and passion for his life's work:

Revealing great, unusual, and remarkable spectacles
opening these to the consideration of every man, and
especially of philosophers and astronomers
as observed by Galileo Galilei
Gentleman of Florence
Professor of Mathematics in the
University of Padua
with the aid of a
spyglass
lately invented by him,
in the surface of the Moon, in innumerable
Fixed Stars, in Nebulae, and above all
in FOUR PLANETS
Swiftly revolving about Jupiter at
differing distances and periods,
and known to no one before the
Author recently perceived them
and decided that they should
be named
THE MEDICEAN STARS

Venice, 1610

Continued Inspiration

Despite the threats of the church, a number of scientists were still very inspired by the work of geniuses such as Galileo. His dedication and persistence, as well as the actual information he discovered, laid the groundwork for others to make amazing discoveries in the fields of astronomy, motion, and energy.

A brilliant scientist born in the same year that Galileo died, 1642, was a dedicated admirer of Galileo. He used much of what the scientist had found out about telescopes in his own research.

Isaac Newton spent much of his time experimenting with air pressure and other issues involved in understanding gravity.

His name was Isaac Newton, an Englishman who attended Cambridge University in the 1660s. He developed a mathematical system called calculus, and he recognized and explained the attractive force between matter, better known as gravity. Later he would refine the telescope, which brought its usefulness to new heights.

Isaac Newton's discoveries changed the way people understood the world around them

Galileo's persistence in developing the telescope and then using it to find out truths about the world around him inspired other scientists. Not only did they build upon the facts he

THREE MEN AND AN IDEA

Galileo's book *The Dialogue Concerning the Two Chief Systems of the World* is considered to be both a scientific and a literary masterpiece. The book discusses the merits of the Ptolemaic and Copernican systems through three main characters. It was written as if two men were having a conversation about the structure of the universe, with a third person listening and making neutral comments.

One of the men in the story is named Filippo Salviati, after one of Galileo's friends. His character is a distinguished man from Florence who strongly believes in the Copernican (i.e., Galileo's) perspectives on a solar system centered on the Sun. A character named

Giovanfranceso Sagredo, also named after a friend, plays the listener from Venice, the observer who hears both sides of the argument. The third character is Simplicio, a person who deeply believes in Aristotle's (i.e., the church's) theories of an Earth-centered solar system. The three men discuss the subject for four whole days. In the end, it is little surprise that the Copernican philosopher wins the day.

The book was approved by the official censor, who requested only that Galileo add a statement that what he wrote was theory, not fact, as he had agreed to do in 1616. He also had to include a statement that made it clear that this book was in opposition to what the Catholic Church believed. He complied with both requirements, and the book was published in February 1632. One thousand copies were printed and sent out. Initial reactions were quite positive. Galileo was praised both for his information and for the entertaining way he delivered it.

The church, however, was not pleased. This book was the last in a series of Galileo's actions that it found to be intolerable. Far too many people were listening to this scientist's ideas, and it was high time to end his popularity. The book was banned within months of being published and remained so for almost two hundred years.

found out but his dedication to his work and his incredible willingness to fight for science in the face of a powerful organization such as the Roman Catholic Church created an excellent model for others.

The development of the telescope and the questions it raised in the minds of scientists and others drove a wedge between the church and its followers. It led to the questioning of traditional beliefs and accepted standards. In the end, however, even the commanding and influential church was not able to put a stop to the overwhelming wave of scientific knowledge that was building.

Sextants were devices used to help calculate a star's position. They used a system of mirrors and prisms.

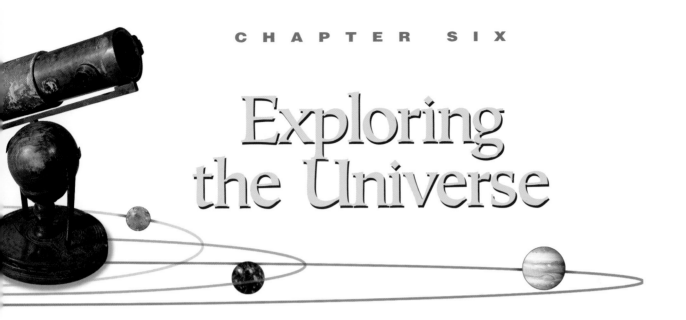

Exploring the Universe

The basic structure of the telescope has not changed much over the centuries, but other modifications have turned the simple, handheld instrument into massive equipment that is capable of more than Galileo could ever have imagined.

In the early 1700s, Sir Isaac Newton made a huge advance in telescope development when he found a solution to a common problem. The refractor telescope used glass lenses inside it. One complication of these lenses was that some of

The telescope fascinated many people. This illustration shows star-watchers using handheld tubes.

55

the bright objects observed had unwanted rings of color added around them. One way to counteract this problem was by making telescopes longer. Some reached more than 100 feet (30 meters) in length.

Early telescopes were built amazingly long in an attempt to get clearer images.

Another problem with glass lenses was their weight. Glass is quite heavy and made telescopes bulky. In addition to this, glass lenses can be supported only from the side, and as they got bigger, gravity distorted the images. Newton handled this by using curved mirrors, creating the first reflector telescope. This allowed telescopes to magnify objects not hundreds of times, but millions of times!

In Newton's reflecting telescope, light from the object being viewed is collected in the primary mirror and reflected to a smaller secondary one.

New Changes, New Faces

In the late 1700s, a German-British composer and amateur astronomer named William Herschel experimented with making his own telescopes. He created a 20-foot (6-m) reflector telescope, which he hung from a pole. He had to climb a ladder to adjust it in any way. In 1781, he made an

Herschel would climb up to his 20-foot telescope and his sister would stand at the base recording his observations as he called them down to her.

enormously important discovery with his telescope—the planet Uranus. When he first spotted the planet, he thought it was a comet. He soon calculated, however, that the object's orbit was not one that a comet would follow. When other scientists began computing its size and orbit, they realized that Herschel had actually discovered another planet within the solar system.

Herschel's discovery led to the finding of yet another planet, Neptune. It was the first planet to be identified through mathematical calculation instead of close observation. They knew it had to exist because of its gravitational effect on the other planets. After many years, several scientists pooled their information and determined that the planet was there. It became official in 1846.

The last planet to be spotted was Pluto. Once again it was by a dedicated amateur astronomer, Clyde Tombaugh. He located the disk in the sky in 1930 at the young age of twenty-four.

Telescope Technology Takes Off

Telescopes continued to get larger and more powerful. In 1917, a man named George Ellery Hale made significant changes in the design of the telescope. He built a 100-inch (254-centimeter) telescope. It was the biggest one in the world for more than thirty years. It was located on Mount Wilson in California. Hale was not satisfied with it, however, so he began designing a 200-inch (508-cm) model. Unfortunately, he wasn't able to finish it before his death in 1938. World War II delayed its completion, but it was finally installed at California's Mount Palomar Observatory for other scientists to use.

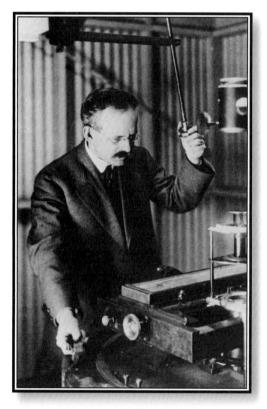

George Ellery Hale was interested in astronomy from an early age. His family supported his passion by purchasing the most up to date telescopes and equipment possible. As an adult he organized the founding of three world-class observatories.

In order to build the 200-inch reflecting telescope, Hale secured a grant for $6 million from the Rockefeller Foundation. Although he did not live long enough to see it built, he was still very proud to be behind the organization to begin its construction.

Completed in 1917, the 100-inch telescope was a difficult and challenging machine. The large mirror was quite sensitive to changes in the temperature and because of that would often go out of focus. Despite this, Hubble would one day use it to discover proof that the universe was continuing to expand.

EDWIN POWELL HUBBLE

Some people are born knowing what they want to do with their lives, and others take a while to figure it out. Edwin Powell Hubble (1889–1953) thought he wanted to be a lawyer. After serving in World War I, he obtained his law degree but had been in practice for only one year before something caught his fancy and led him in a new direction—astronomy.

Hubble began working at Mount Wilson Observatory just outside Pasadena, California, in the San Gabriel Mountains. There he learned quickly and eventually gathered data that would change how scientists and the world would look at outer space. He realized that the distant, faint clouds of light called nebulae that telescopes were spotting in the sky are actually other galaxies, just like the Milky Way that Earth is in. This concept made everyone suddenly aware of how utterly vast the universe is and that there are endless possibilities of what is out there. This was a huge discovery.

In 1929, at the age of forty, Hubble made the biggest discovery of his lifetime. He determined that the farther away a galaxy is from the Milky Way, the faster it moves away. With this observation he developed a theory of an expanding universe. This new and startling idea eventually led to the theory of the "Big Bang," which states that the universe began in one instant about 14 billion years ago.

Today one of the world's most powerful telescopes is named for Edwin Powell Hubble.

Hubble and Beyond

With little doubt, one of the most impressive telescopes ever built is the *Hubble Space Telescope* (*HST*). The project was a joint effort of the European Space Agency and the American National Aeronautics and Space Administration (NASA). It took years to develop.

HST is 43.5 feet (13 m) long, the size of a school bus. It cost $2.2 billion to construct. On Earth it weighs 24,500 pounds (11,110 kilograms), or as much as two elephants. The main mirror inside this telescope is 7 feet 10 inches (2.5 m)! Sir Isaac Newton would have been amazed!

Five astronauts aboard the space shuttle *Discovery* officially deployed the HST on April 25, 1990. It orbits Earth 380 times each day transmitting enough information to fill 10,000 floppy computer disks. That is the equivalent of five encyclopedias! *HST's* mission

Launching the Hubble Space Telescope *from the space shuttle* Endeavour *went smoothly. A few days later, NASA discovered a problem with its giant mirror and it took three years before it could be captured and repaired.*

FROM IDEAS TO REALITY

A telescope in outer space? It is a common idea now, but it was totally foreign when Lyman Spitzer Jr. (1914–1997) first suggested it. Spitzer was a theoretical astrophysicist. In 1946, he proposed the concept of developing a large telescopic observatory in space. There it could examine space without the distortion of Earth's atmosphere getting in the way. This unusual idea eventually morphed into the *HST*.

Spitzer played an important role in the design and development of the *HST*. During the 1960s and 1970s, he was also a spokesperson and advocate of the instrument both in Congress and to the scientific community. He continued to support the Hubble project and to analyze the unique data that came from the telescope until his death in 1997 at the age of eighty-three.

description includes exploring the solar system and measuring the universe to determine its age and size.

Since its initial launch, the *HST* has made some astounding discoveries. In 1994 it witnessed a once-in-a-millennium occurrence when fragments of a comet entered Jupiter's atmosphere and exploded. *HST* has recorded a number of star births and deaths. It has probed the centers of galaxies and found that many contain "eating machines" called **black holes**. It has also captured enormous cosmic explosions.

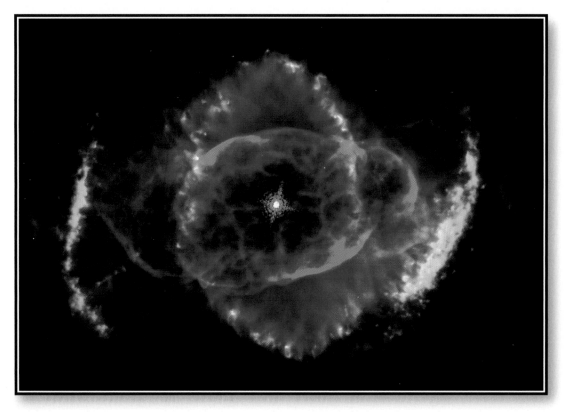

The Cat's Eye Nebula was captured by the Hubble Space Telescope *on March 24, 2002. It shows the evolution of a dying star throwing off shells of glowing gas.*

The Hubble *has captured some amazing photos over the years, including a black hole–powered core of a nearby active galaxy.*

One of the instrument's most amazing discoveries, however, was that the universe does not remain still. Instead, it continues to expand at very fast rates. In May 1999, a team of astronomers came up with a profoundly complex equation to determine the age of the universe—between 12 and 14 billion years old!

As successful and high-tech as the *HST* is, there is another project waiting in the wings that is even more advanced. It is called the *James Webb Space Telescope* (*JWST*), formerly known as the *Next Generation Space Telescope*. It will

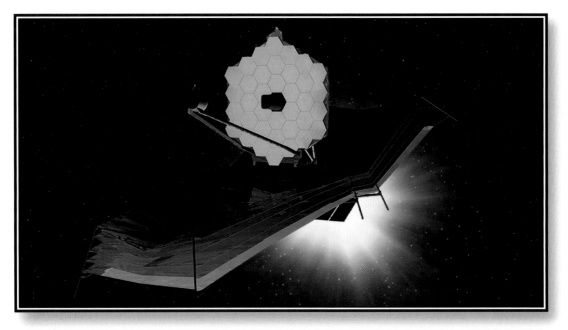

This is an artist's concept of the James Webb Space Telescope. *Its mission will be to determine the shape of the universe and understand the birth and death of stars.*

have the largest mirror ever installed in a telescope and is expected to have ten times more light-gathering ability than the *HST's* mirror. NASA plans to launch it in 2011. The *JWST* is destined to make some awesome discoveries. It has been designed to look way back in time at the universe's first stars and to examine galaxies and how they evolved.

The push to find new and more useful designs for the telescope continues today. Already, X-ray telescopes and radio telescopes are being used to record energy coming from stars and other celestial objects. It should not be long before discoveries from these instruments amaze the world, just as that first telescope did.

The Chandra Space Observatory is the third of NASA's great observatories. It allows scientists to get x-ray images across huge distances.

From that very first thought that humans might see farther than their eyes would allow to creating the complicated software that will help to control the *JWST*, the motivation is the same: the drive to know more about the universe.

What lies within this vast, expanding universe? What planets have not yet been discovered? What life forms may be out there, peering at Earth with their own instruments? Such questions continue to fascinate and inspire scientists the same way they did long ago. Most likely, they will continue to do so for years and years to come.

The Telescope: A Timeline

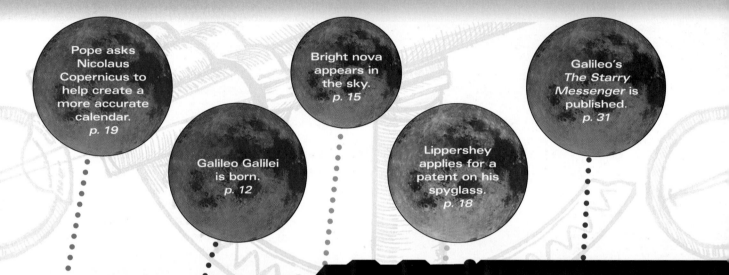

Pope asks Nicolaus Copernicus to help create a more accurate calendar.
p. 19

Galileo Galilei is born.
p. 12

Bright nova appears in the sky.
p. 15

Lippershey applies for a patent on his spyglass.
p. 18

Galileo's *The Starry Messenger* is published.
p. 31

1514 1543 1564 1570 1572 1604 1608 1609 1610 1632

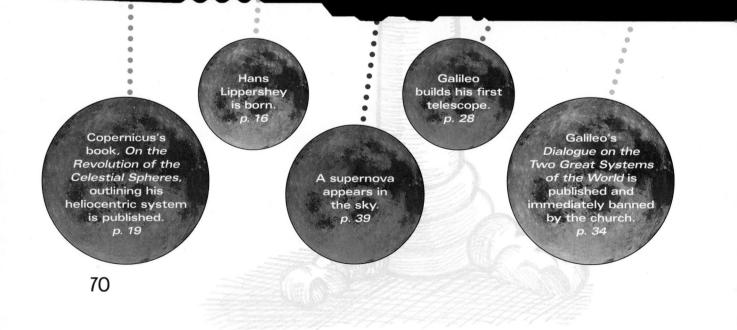

Copernicus's book, *On the Revolution of the Celestial Spheres*, outlining his heliocentric system is published.
p. 19

Hans Lippershey is born.
p. 16

A supernova appears in the sky.
p. 39

Galileo builds his first telescope.
p. 28

Galileo's *Dialogue on the Two Great Systems of the World* is published and immediately banned by the church.
p. 34

Galileo is convicted of heresy by the Roman Catholic Church and sentenced to house arrest.
p. 36

Sir Issac Newton invents the reflecting telescope.
p. 57

The ban on Galileo's *Dialogue on the Two Great Systems of the World* is finally lifted.
p. 53

Lyman Spitzer Jr. suggests putting a telescope in outer space.
p. 63

The Roman Catholic Church pardons Galileo.
p. 37

1633   1642   1704   1781   1882   1917   1946   1990   1992   2011

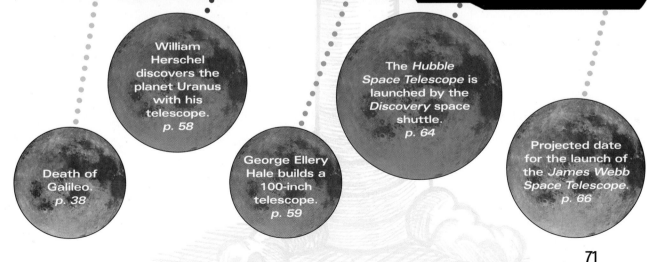

Death of Galileo.
p. 38

William Herschel discovers the planet Uranus with his telescope.
p. 58

George Ellery Hale builds a 100-inch telescope.
p. 59

The *Hubble Space Telescope* is launched by the *Discovery* space shuttle.
p. 64

Projected date for the launch of the *James Webb Space Telescope*.
p. 66

71

Glossary

black hole: An area in space where mass is so dense that its gravitational pull cannot be resisted; anything that enters can never escape

cartographer: Mapmaker

constellation: An arrangement of groups of stars

galaxy: A large system of gas, dust, and millions or billions of stars, such as the Milky Way

geocentric: Earth-centered perspective; the idea that the objects in the solar system revolve around Earth

heliocentric: Sun-centered perspective; the idea that the Earth and other planets revolve around the Sun

heresy: An opinion or doctrine that is controversial and/or contrary to the church's doctrine

72

Inquisition: An inquiry and trial by the Roman Catholic Church dedicated to punishing heresy

nova: A star that suddenly and temporarily becomes much brighter

orbiting: Revolving around

patent: An official document securing the exclusive right to make, use, or sell an invention

pendulum: An object suspended from a fixed point that swings back and forth under the influence of gravity at fixed intervals

protuberance: Something that protrudes, or sticks out or up

Renaissance: Period of time from the mid-fourteenth to the end of the sixteenth century during which there was a rebirth of interest in the arts and science

sinuosity: Something that has a wavy or winding form

supernova: A catastrophic explosion that occurs at the end of the life of a very massive star

To Find Out More

Books

MacLachlan, James. *Galilei: First Physics.* New York: Oxford University Press, 1997.

Sis, Peter. *Starry Messenger.* New York: Fararr, Straus and Giroux, 1996.

Swisher, Clarice. *Galileo. San Deigo, CA:* Greenhaven Press, 2001.

Voit, Mark. *Hubble Space Telescope: New Views of the Universe.* New York: Harry N. Abrams, 2000.

White, Michael. *Galileo Galilei: Inventor, Astronomer, and Rebel.* Woodbridge, Conn.: Blackbirch Press, 1999.

Zannos, Susan. *Edwin Hubble and the Theory of the Expanding Universe (Unlocking the Secrets of Science).* Hockessin, DE: Mitchell Lane Publishers, 2003.

Web Sites

Hubble Space Telescope
http://hubblesite.org/
Web site for the Hubble telescope, information on the history of the telescope, and general discussion about the solar system

Galileo and the Telescope
http://csep10.phys.utk.edu/astr161/lect/history/galileo.html
This site offers information on the history of the telescope, as well as the story of Galileo and his many experiments

Galileo's Biography
http://es.rice.edu/ES/humsoc/Galileo/Bio/
Web site that focuses on Galileo's life from beginning to end

Organizations

Goddard Space Flight Center
Code 130 Office of Public Affairs
Greenbelt, MD 20771

Mount Wilson Institute
c/o CHARA
Georgia State University
MSC 8R0320
One Park Place, Suite 720
Atlanta, GA 30303-3088

Index

About the Author

Tamra Orr is a freelance writer living in Portland, Oregon. She specializes in writing nonfiction books for children and families and is the author of more than thirty books. For Franklin Watts she wrote *Violence in Our Schools: Halls of Hope, Halls of Fear* and for Children's Press she wrote Enchantment of the World, *Turkey* and *Slovenia*.

In order to write this book, Orr surfed the Web, and in doing so found some fascinating and informative sites. She read a number of books about history and invention and developed a real affection for Galileo. In addition, she dusted off her husband's telescope and examined it. She identified the parts and then spent several nights looking through it and learning firsthand about focus—and patience. Orr has an all-new respect for Galileo and cannot imagine how he could have spent so many long hours looking up!